P9-CEN-428

Please remember that this is a library book,
and that it belongs only temporarily to each
person who uses it. Be considerate. Do
not write in this, or any, library book.

WITHDRAWN

WITHDRAWN

AAW-1071

VC-Liberalism

Learning Style Theory and Practice

JAMES W. KEEFE

WITHDRAWN

National Association of Secondary School Principals
1904 Association Drive, Reston, Virginia 22091

James W. Keefe is director of research for the
National Association of Secondary School Principals
and coauthor of the NASSP Learning Style Profile.

Executive Director:	Scott D. Thomson
Director of Publications:	Thomas F. Koerner
Editor:	Patricia Lucas George
Technical Editor:	Eugenia Cooper Potter

Copyright 1987
All Rights Reserved
ISBN 0-88210-201-X

National Association of Secondary School Principals
1904 Association Drive, Reston, Virginia 22091
(703) 860-0200

Contents

Foreword

THE EL DORADO FOR EDUCATORS, reaching back to the early transformation of "school" from tutorials to group instruction, has been to discover the way to teach individual students in a common setting. After 2,500 years, we are still only marginally successful in this quest.

If we fall short, it is not for lack of effort. Particularly since the advent of John Dewey we Americans have made herculean efforts to accommodate the learner and to acknowledge individual differences in students. We have insisted that learning be "meaningful" and that school is a society of young people as well as a place to encounter content.

But we have only faintly understood the learner even as we accommodated school to the social disposition of children and youth. Often we adjusted the school setting with new formats ranging from nongraded instruction to team teaching to open classrooms. Often we tinkered with new technical tools, including aptitude tests and teaching machines and visual devices. They all helped, a little, but none dramatically.

Much of this well-intended experimentation failed to focus on the unique learning proclivities of individual students. For example, schools "individualized" instruction by providing independent study time for all students, even though some students need structure to learn. We could easily make a long list of these contradictions created with the best of intentions. We do know now, however, that no single approach to instruction is adequate.

We have learned that effective instructional planning must accommodate the learning characteristics of individual students to be effective with these students. We also have seen that understanding the learner requires more than just conventional wisdom about the ways students process information. Hence the decade-long interest of the NASSP in learning style and brain behavior.

This monograph builds upon rapid developments in the field during the past few years. It provides useful information about the theory, research, instrumentation, and practice of learning style. It is highly readable and will be immensely useful to all educators seriously interested in broadening their understanding of the ways students learn. It proves that valuable things do indeed come in small packages.

I would like to commend Jim Keefe, the director of research for NASSP and author of this monograph, for his tenacious and creative efforts to improve our understanding of students and the complexities of their learning. This understanding, as it grows, is the key to effective teaching and hence to effective schools. I would also like to express my appreciation to the members of NASSP's Learning Styles Task Force for their commitment to our collective quest to focus instructional improvement efforts upon a deeper understanding of the information-processing patterns of individual students.

Scott D. Thomson
Executive Director, NASSP

CHAPTER 1

Learning Style: An Overview

LEARNING IS A FASCINATING INTERACTIVE process, the product of student and teacher activity within a specific learning environment. These activities, which are central elements of the learning process, show wide variation in pattern, style, and quality. In reality, however, the process in many schools has not changed much over the years. And the public, the press, and even many in the profession have a generally simplistic view of the relationship between the process and student achievement.

Many educators think of instruction and learning as directly related. If the one is present to an acceptable degree, the other should naturally follow. If the teacher is working hard, students should learn. If they do not, an earlier generation blamed the student while the current trend is to hold the teachers, administrator, and school accountable. The reality again is considerably more complex.

Consider these scenarios.

John is a junior at Metro High School. He is a quiet, well-mannered young man, generally accepted by his peers and liked by his teachers. He arrived at the high school with the reputation of being a good student and hard worker. Yet, his grades have gone down every semester since coming to Metro. He is ill-prepared to function in the prevailing environment of the high school. He seems to need more structure to achieve, the kind of atmosphere that his junior high school specialized in. His teachers have advised him, given him special attention, even chastized him for a lack of self-direction. He continues to lose ground.

Mary is a seventh grader. She attends the same junior high from which John graduated. It is a traditional, teacher-centered school of self-contained classrooms and limited curriculum. Everything runs smoothly in an environment dominated by structure and order. Both of Mary's parents are educators who have raised her to be her own person. They have encouraged her to do well in school and have difficulty understanding why she has not responded. Mary always seems to be in trouble. She finds the junior high wearisome and the teachers well-meaning but unhelpful. Faculty members seem to have their own agendas. They do not appear to understand Mary's adjustment problems.

Neither student is learning to ability. The fault clearly does not lie with the student, the teachers, or the home alone, but is the result of conflicting forces. It is a case of a student in the wrong place; and ultimately, of inflexible approaches to instruction.

The School Learning Process

Kurt Lewin noted that behavior is a function of the person and the environment. Three interacting factors influence the learning process — the student, the instructor, and the school environment. If any of these factors is unsynchronized, the process can falter. John and Mary were unwitting and unwilling victims of a well-meaning system. Neither the school nor their parents recognized the mismatch between student style, teacher style, and the predominant learning structure. Student behavior was dysfunctional because persons and environment were out of step.

The emphasis in schools has changed from decade to decade. In the 1930s, progressive educators concentrated on the needs of the child. In the 1940s, a nation at war developed a curriculum that was society-centered. In the 1950s and early 1960s, scholars led the way toward a "structure of the (subject) discipline" approach. In the late 1960s and early 1970s the total curriculum came into focus with an emphasis on the humane in schools. The late 1970s brought basic skills and educational accountability as the major themes. There is great need today for a unifying model amid this continuing search for a better way.

Benjamin Bloom (1976) proposed a significant model of school learning. His theory deals with three important elements: student characteristics, instruction, and learning outcomes. Bloom's thesis is that there are three interdependent variables that account for the greatest degree of variance in student learning. These variables are:

1. Cognitive entry behaviors — the extent to which the student has already learned the basic prerequisites to the learning to be undertaken

2. Affective entry characteristics — the extent to which the student is or can be motivated to engage in the learning process

3. Quality of instruction — the extent to which the instruction to be provided is appropriate to the learner.

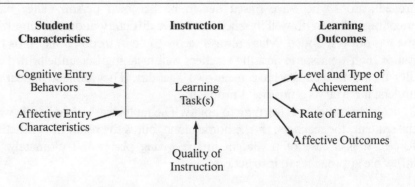

Figure 1. Bloom's variables in the theory of school learning

Bloom hypothesized that when cognitive and affective entry behaviors and quality of instruction are appropriate, learning will be at a high level and student outcomes will vary little. When student entry characteristics and instructional quality are more variable, learning outcomes will vary accordingly. Differences in level and type of student learning, then, are determined by the students' learning history and the quality of the instructional setting.

Bloom and his colleagues spent a great deal of time researching the effects of student cognitive and affective entry behaviors. There seems to be little doubt that the prior knowledge and skills a student brings to new learning and attitudes toward self, school, and subject account for most of learning effectiveness. When prior learning is deficient, the school's job is primarily remedial. When motivation is lacking, counseling and a measure of success are the answers. But the school can make its most significant ongoing contribution in the area of instructional quality. Here, early diagnosis and appropriate prescription are the keys to effectiveness.

Experienced educators know that the quality of instruction is greatly influenced by the particular mix of student characteristics, teacher approach, and classroom organization. Bloom's model looks at school learning primarily from the instructional perspective. It deals with prior learning and motivation, the nature of the learning task(s), and indicators of learning effectiveness. It is not directly concerned with the wide variety of approaches that a teacher may utilize in creating a learning environment. Nor does it consider the range of diagnostic information needed to respond to student differences. In particular, it overlooks stylistic variations. It is the object of this volume to propose a model of student learning styles and to discuss various applications in current research and school practice.

The Learning Style Concept

Learning styles are characteristic cognitive, affective, and physiological behaviors that serve as relatively stable indicators of how learners perceive, interact with, and respond to the learning environment (NASSP, 1979).

Because learning is an internal process, we know that it has taken place only when we observe a change of learner behavior of a more or less permanent nature resulting from what has been experienced. Similarly, we can recognize the learning style of an individual student only by observing his or her overt behavior. Learning style is a consistent way of functioning that reflects the underlying causes of learning behavior.

As Gregorc (1979) suggested, "Style appears to be both nature/ nurture in its roots. Patterns of adapting to environments are apparently available to us through our genetic coding system . . . through our environment and culture . . . (and) within the subjective part of our individual natures." Styles are hypothetical constructs that help to explain the learning (and teaching) process. They are qualities in the behavior of individual learners that persist regardless of the teaching methods or content experienced.

Learning style and cognitive style have often been used synonymously in the literature although they decidedly are not the same. Learning style, in fact, is the broader term and includes cognitive along with affective and physiological styles. This distinction and relationship will become clearer in the course of this discussion.

Elements of learning style appeared in the research literature as early as 1892. Most of that early research (before 1940) concerned the relationship between memory and oral or visual teaching methods. The findings were conflicting, no doubt due in large part to the differences in the populations, learning materials, and test instrumentation that were utilized.

Most early researchers were too preoccupied with finding the one perceptual mode that would best increase learning or retention. Even before 1900, Cattell and Jostrow attempted to relate differences in perceptual mode to general intelligence and learning performance without success. Vernon, Eysench, and others described perceptual typologies such as analyzers vs. synthesizers and color vs. form reactors.

The term "cognitive style" was coined by Allport in 1937 to refer to a quality of living and adapting influenced by distinctive personality types. In the 1940s, Thurstone and later Guilford identified factors of perceptual speed and flexibility (through the techniques of factor analysis) which they believed were related to personality.

Specific research on cognitive styles was greatly expanded after World War II at Brooklyn College, the Menninger Foundation, and the Fels Institute. Asch and Witkin at Brooklyn College worked with the bi-polar trait of "field dependence-independence," the ability of a person to identify a figure against a background field. In time, Witkin and his associates broadened this notion to include "analytic-global" functions and the concept of "psychological differentiation."

Holzman, Gardner, and others at the Menninger group concentrated on cognitive style as a complexus of cognitive controls. At the Fels Institute, Kagan and his colleagues focused on analytic styles of thinking and problem solving. Research on analytic and non-analytic modes led to the identification of a "reflection-impulsivity" dimension. The reflective person tends to analyze and thoroughly differentiate a complex concept; an impulsive person is inclined to make quick and often erroneous responses.

Although differences in criterion tests used to measure the variables make comparisons a bit shaky, Davis (1967) saw a similar active-passive dimension in the work of the Brooklyn, Menninger, and Fels groups, as follows:

Active Analysis		Passive Acceptance
Field independence	(Witkin)	Field dependence
Differentiation	(Gardner)	Undifferentiation
Reflection	(Kagan)	Impulsivity

The consideration of cognitive style widened after 1960 to include selection strategies (scanning and focusing), open/closed mindedness, memory or retention styles, risk taking vs. cautiousness, and sensory modality preferences (kinesthetic, visual, and auditory).

Current efforts to explain the underlying processes of learning and teaching reflect two lines of research. One group is working with applied models of learning style (e.g., Hill, 1976; Hunt et al., 1978; Dunn and Dunn, 1978). Interview techniques or self-report questionnaires are used to identify student perceptions of their own characteristic traits.

The other line of research retains a strong preference for the cognitive style dimension. An early example is the model developed by McKenney and his associates (1974) at the Harvard Business School. This model is bidimensional rather than simply bi-polar. For McKenney, human information processing has two dimensions: information gathering (perceptive vs. receptive) and information evaluating (systematic vs. intuitive). Gregorc (1979) and Letteri (1980) have developed school-related cognitive models. These approaches will be discussed in Chapter 2.

The term "learning style" was probably first used by Thelen (1954) in discussing the dynamics of groups at work. The term has been conceptualized in several ways since that time. The model of learning style proposed in this chapter views style as having three dimensions: 1) cognitive, 2) affective, and 3) physiological.

COGNITIVE STYLES

Cognitive styles are "information processing habits representing the learner's typical mode of perceiving, thinking, problem solving, and remembering" (Messick, 1976). As our brief review of the learning style movement has indicated, the vast majority of research on personality-related learning variables has been in the area of cognitive style. Each learner has preferred ways of perception, organization, and retention that are distinctive and consistent. These characteristic differences are called cognitive styles. Styles are aptitudes or traits of the individual, functioning personality.

Cognitive styles are related to, but different from, intellectual abilities. The latter are usually referred to by such terms as general intelligence, mental ability, scholastic ability, I.Q., or even aptitude. Notable differences exist between styles and abilities (Messick et al., 1976). Abilities deal with the content of cognition; they tell what kind of information is being processed by what operation in what form. Styles, on the other hand, illustrate the process of cognition; they tell *how* information is being processed. Abilities measure specific innate capacities and are value directional — more of an ability is better than less. Styles are controlling mechanisms concerned with the manner or preference of performance and are value differentiated — each extreme may be learning-adaptive depending on the circumstances.

Some common ground exists between abilities and styles. Cognitive fluency and flexibility (abilities) and complexity vs. simplicity (styles) appear to fall somewhere between ability and style. Both are basically bi-polar with differentiated value attached to the extremes depending on the circumstances, yet greater value is ordinarily attached to one pole of the dimension than to the other. Greater fluency and complexity are usually more highly valued.

Messick et al. (1976) list more than 20 dimensions of cognitive style that are derived from experimental research. Some of these elements are straightforward in their meaning and implication; others are very complex. It is possible to organize the style dimensions in a general way as they touch on either reception or concept formation and retention. Reception styles are concerned with the perception and analysis of data. Concept formation and retention styles deal with hypothesis generation, problem solving, and memory processing.

Reception Styles

1. *Perceptual modality preferences* — preferred reliance on one of the sensory modes for understanding experience. The typical modes are kinesthetic or psychomotor, visual or spatial, and auditory or verbal. Preference seems to evolve from kinesthetic in childhood to visual and eventually verbal in later years. In adults, all three modes function cooperatively with a usually discernible preference for one or the other. (Bruner, Oliver, and Greenfield, 1966; Sperry, 1973; Messick et al., 1976)

2. *Field independence vs. dependence* — analytical as opposed to non-analytical way of experiencing the environment. Independents perceive things as distinct from their background field, while dependents tend to be influenced by any embedding context. This style perhaps has been the subject of more research than any other. (Witkin et al., 1954)

3. *Scanning* — differences in the way individuals focus attention. Attention may be broad or narrow and a person's style may be to scan or focus. The scanning or extensiveness dimension has received more attention from researchers than the focusing or intensity elements. (Gardner and Long, 1962; Holzman, 1966)

4. *Constricted vs. flexible control* — individual differences in susceptibility to distraction and distortion in tasks with conflicting cues. The constricted style is more susceptible to distraction while the flexible style tends to concentrate on the task at hand. (Gardner et al., 1959)

5. *Tolerance for incongruous or unrealistic experiences* — readiness to accept perceptions at variance with conventional experience. A high tolerance style reflects a willingness to accept experiences that vary markedly from the ordinary (or even the truth). Low tolerance implies a preference for conventional ideas. (Gardner et al., 1959)

6. *Strong vs. weak automatization* — the capacity to perform simple repetitive tasks. Relative skill in performing simple tasks has been found to run contrary to relative skill in perceptual analysis, suggesting an intra-personal style of automatization vs. restructuring. Learners with a strong automatization style appear to concentrate on the obvious properties of a task, ignoring the details that restructuring requires. (Broverman, 1960a, 1960b)

7. *Conceptual vs. perceptual* — the capability to perform novel or difficult tasks. Conceptual learners show greater facility for conceptual behavior and less for perceptual-motor ones. Perceptually dominant individuals exhibit the opposite pattern. (Broverman, 1960a, 1960b)

Concept Formation and Retention Styles

1. *Conceptual tempo* — individual differences in the speed and adequacy of hypothesis formulation and information processing on a continuum of reflection vs. impulsivity. Impulsives tend to give the first answer they can think of even though it is often incorrect. Reflectives prefer to consider alternate solutions before deciding and to give more reasoned responses. (Kagan, 1966)

2. *Conceptualizing styles* — individual differences in approach to concept formation. Conceptual differentiation characterizes learners who conceive of things as having many properties rather than a few. Compartmentalization characterizes those who place concepts in discrete, even relatively rigid categories. The chief conceptualizing bases are the use of thematic or functional relations among stimuli (relational conceptualizing), the analysis of descriptive attributes (analytic-descriptive conceptualizing), or the inference of categorical membership (categorical-inferential conceptualizing). (Kagan, Moss, and Sigel, 1963)

3. *Breadth of categorizing* — preference for broad or narrow range in establishing conceptual categories. The broad categorizer likes to include many items and lessen the risk of leaving something out. The narrow categorizer prefers to exclude doubtful items and lessen the probability of including something that does not fit. (Pettigrew, 1958)

4. *Cognitive complexity vs. simplicity* — differences in number of dimensions utilized by individuals to construe the world. A high complexity style is multi-dimensional and discriminating, accepting of diversity and conflict. A low complexity style likes consistency and regularity in the environment. The former is more effective in processing conflicting information; the latter in reconciling similar experiences. Harvey and his colleagues refer to this dimension as abstract vs. concrete. (Bieri, 1961; Scott, 1962)

5. *Leveling vs. sharpening* — individual variations in memory processing. Levelers tend to blur similar memories and to merge new experiences readily with previous ones; they tend to over-generalize. Sharpeners are able to distinguish small differences and to separate memory of prior experiences more easily from current ones; they tend to over-discriminate. (Gardner et al., 1959; Holzman and Gardner, 1960)

AFFECTIVE STYLES

The second dimension of learning style encompasses those aspects of personality that have to do with attention, emotion, and valuing. Motivation includes the processes of arousal, expectancy, and incentive. Arousal describes the general level of attention and responsiveness of an organism.

Optimum attention is ordinarily an intermediate level between boredom and excitement. Arousal involves traits such as curiosity, exploratory behavior, boredom, anxiety, and frustration.

The strength of a person's action is a product of both expectancy and valence. Expectancy is the subjective certainty that a particular outcome will follow a particular act, that something will or will not occur. Anticipated satisfaction (valence) is associated with expectancy. A learner strives for whatever he desires greatly (valence) and has high hope of success (expectancy). Achievement motivation (the "motive to achieve") is an example of both expectancy and satisfaction in mastering challenging tasks. Incentives (rewards) are typical expectancies.

Motivation is the end product of attention, valuing, and incentive. *Affective learning styles are the offshoots of these same motivational processes viewed as the learner's typical mode of arousing, directing, and sustaining behavior.* As with cognitive style, affective style is a hypothetical construct. We cannot directly observe affective style, only infer it from a person's interaction with the enrivonment.

Affective style is not the same as motivation; motivation is one of its determinants. Affective style is relatively consistent for a given learner in a given environment. Individual motivational responses may vary but the learner's affective style will remain fairly stable over a reasonable period of time.

Obviously, there is a large subjective component in all this. Ball (1977) put it succinctly:

> A teacher sees a student as motivated if the student wants to do, and does, those things the teacher thinks the student should do. By the same token, a student is seen by the teacher as unmotivated if the student will not do, or has to be made to do, those things that a teacher thinks the student should do.

Affective style is the result of motivational processes that are subject to a wide variety of influences. The learner is affected by the cultural environment, parental and peer pressures, school influences, and personality factors. Values are involved. Not every student can be successful in every learning environment because accustomed habits may prove to be at odds with school values. Diagnosis of affective learning style is critical, then, to effective school learning.

It is useful to classify the many dimensions of affective style according to some general scheme. We will use the elements of attention and expectancy/incentive as the basis for our classification. Placement in the categories is by no means definitive; certainly some conceptual overlap exists among the styles. The basis for determination is the dominant focus of the affective trait(s) emphasized in the style.

Attention Styles

1. *Conceptual level* — a broad developmental trait characterizing how much structure a student requires in order to learn best. CL is "based on a

developmental personality theory that describes persons on a developmental hierarchy of increasing conceptual complexity, self-responsibility, and independence" (Hunt et al., 1978). A low conceptual level style indicates the need for high structure; a high CL indicates that the learner requires less structure.

Conceptual level is a broad trait and is classified here mainly because of its developmental implications. Closely related to it are *responsibility,* the capacity of students to follow through on a task without direct or frequent supervision, and *need for structure,* the amount and kind of structure required by different individuals. (Hunt et al., 1978; Dunn and Dunn, 1978)

2. *Curiosity* — differences in attraction to the novel or adventuresome aspects of the environment. Curiosity includes exploratory behavior, reactions to changes or the need for change, and efforts to escape boredom. Not all psychologists agree about the nature of curiosity, but it does seem to grow out of the perception of some kind of discrepancy in the environment. (Berlyne, 1954)

3. *Persistence or perseverance* — variations in learner's willingness to labor beyond the required time, to withstand the discomfort, and to face the prospect of failure. High persistence is characterized by the disposition to work at a task until it is completed, seeking whatever kind of help is necessary to persevere. A low persistence style results in short attention span and the inability to work on a task for any length of time. (Carroll, 1963)

4. *Level of anxiety* — describes the individual's level of apprehension and tension under stress conditions. The highly anxious are tense and worried; the unanxious are emotionally "cool." A low anxious learner performs better when challenged by a difficult task, particularly when the performance will be evaluated. A high anxious learner performs less well under these same conditions. Some evidence exists that the highly intelligent profit more from anxiety than the less able. (Alpert and Haber, 1960; Spielberger, 1966)

5. *Frustration tolerance* — individual differences in thwarting behavior in the face of conflict or disappointment. Learners low in frustration tolerance are more likely to extend effort in a conflict situation — to accept the challenge. (Waterhouse and Child, 1953)

Expectancy and Incentive Styles
1. *Locus of control* — variations in individual perceptions of causality on a continuum of internality vs. externality. The internal person thinks of himself as responsible for his own behavior, as deserving praise for successes and blame for failures. The external person sees circumstances beyond his control, luck, or other people as responsible for his behavior. Some evidence suggests that a greater sense of internality can be developed. (Rotter, 1966, 1971; Crandall, Katkovsky, and Crandall, 1965)

2. *Achievement motivation* — individual differences in patterns of planning and striving for some internalized standard of excellence. Individuals with high achievement motivation are interested in excellence for its own sake rather than for any rewards it may bring. They set their goals carefully, after calculating the probability of success of a variety of alternatives. This style is also called *need for achievement* (n-Ach). (McClelland et al., 1955; Alschuler, 1973)

3. *Self-actualization* — differences in personal striving for adequacy. Maslow and other humanistic psychologists view life as a "continual series of choices for the individual in which the main determinant of choice is the person as he already *is* (including his goals for himself, his courage or fear, his feeling of responsibility, his ego-strength or 'willpower,' etc.)" The more actualized person has a greater feeling of "adequacy." (Maslow, 1968)

4. *Imitation* — the tendency to repeat actions that appear desirable in a given situation. The young, in particular, identify with role models and tend to imitate what they say and do. Imitative behavior seems to depend on the perceived personality of the model, the personality of the learner, and the interaction between the two factors. (Bandura, 1962; Kagan, 1958)

5. *Risk taking vs. cautiousness* — individual differences in a person's willingness to take chances to achieve some goal. Risk takers prefer low probability-high payoff alternatives; cautious persons like high probability-low payoff ones. (Kogan and Wallach, 1964)

6. *Competition vs. cooperation* — tendency of individuals to be motivated more by rivalry or by the sharing of experience. In solving various problems, Deutsch (1960) found cooperative groups superior in almost every respect, but the group is not necessarily any more successful than the best problem solver in it. The highly competitive have a strong compulsion to win; the highly cooperative, a strong need to agree and support. (Maccoby, 1972)

7. *Level of aspiration* — variations in learner perception of past successes and failures in relation to subsequent school performance. Bloom (1976) and his colleagues term this style *academic self-concept*. Past successes tend to develop modest self-confidence while failure can lead either to despair or to an unrealistic optimism born out of defeat. Those who fail often tend to develop a mind set ranging from a lowered level of expectancy to the need to discredit the evidence of failure. (Bachman, 1964; Brookover, Shailer, and Peterson, 1964)

8. *Reaction to reinforcement* — individual differences in response to reward and punishment. A positive reinforcer is some kind of reward (e.g., praise, prizes, money). A negative reinforcer is the removal of an unpleasant state or event (e.g., threat of punishment, scolding). Punishment is the removal of reward and the addition of an aversive stimulus. Generally speaking, students are motivated by reinforcement and variable in response to punishment. (Skinner, 1953)

9. *Social motivation* — differences in value-based behavior based on variations in social and racial/ethnic world view. Learners not only vary in
socioeconomic background, cultural determinants and value codes, and
peer-group conformity, but are variously affected by the standards and
expectations of these groups. Esthetic sense, for example, is strongly
influenced by social and ethnic background. Value systems arise out of
family, school, and peer-group influences. Differences in social motivation
may derive from one or a combination of determinants. (Riessman, 1962;
Hill, 1976)

10. *Personal interests* — patterns of choice among alternatives that do not
seem to result from external pressures. All else being equal, an individual
who has an interest in something is likely to favor it over its alternatives.
High interest will incline a learner toward an activity; low interest, away
from it. (Witty, 1961)

PHYSIOLOGICAL STYLES

The final grouping of learning styles describes the characteristic learning-related behaviors of the human body. *Physiological styles are biologically-based modes of response that are founded on sex-related differences,
personal nutrition and health, and accustomed reaction to the physical environment.* Physiological factors are among the most evident influences in
the process of school learning. The student who is hungry, ill, or malnour-
ished behaves differently than the youngster who is healthy. Males and
females respond differently in certain learning situations. All learners are
affected by the physical environment of the school.

The small number and more obvious nature of the physiological
factors make any additional basis for classification unnecessary.

1. *Sex-related behavior* — variations in typical learning responses of males
and females. Researchers agree that males generally are more aggressive
and more sensitive to spatial (visual) relations and (perhaps) to mathematical processes. Females are more verbal and excel in fine muscular control.
The sexes display differing attentional mechanisms and widely varying
interest patterns. Sex-related differences may or may not be innate or
related to brain hemispheric preferences. In any case, their pervasive
influence makes their consideration imperative. (Maccoby and Jacklin,
1974; Wittig and Peterson, 1979)

2. *Health-related behavior* — individual response variations arising from
good health or from malnutrition, hunger, and disease. Dunn and Dunn
refer to an aspect of this style as *intake.* No widely accepted measures of
these factors exist and the many potential implications for learning can
only be surmised because of the clumsiness of the available methodology.
Yet it is clear that the differences do exist. (Cravioto, 1971; Dunn and
Dunn, 1978)

3. *Time-of-day rhythms* — individual differences in learning response
depending on the time of day. Some persons perform best in the morning;

others in the afternoon or evening. These differences likely reflect early childhood sleeping patterns and the circadian rhythms of the body. (Dermer and Berscheid, 1972; Dunn and Dunn, 1978)

4. *Need for mobility* — differences in learner need for change in posture and location. This dimension may be both age and sex-linked, since younger learners and males generally require more mobility. (Fitt, 1975; Dunn and Dunn, 1978)

5. *Environmental elements* — individual preference for, or response to, varying levels of light, sound, and temperature. Few learners are greatly bothered by light variations but many find it hard to work with distracting noise levels, and wide temperature variations affect almost everyone. (Dunn and Dunn, 1978)

Summary

The school learning process reflects the interaction of student cognitive and affective behaviors and the organization of the instructional environment. School reform efforts of the 1970s and 1980s have moved the purposes and importance of effective instruction to the forefront of American education. Learning style analysis emerges as a key element in this movement to make learning and instruction more responsive to the needs of individual students.

We have defined learning styles in this larger context as characteristic cognitive, affective, and physiological behaviors that serve as relatively stable indicators of how learners perceive, interact with, and respond to the learning environment. Cognitive styles are information-processing habits; affective styles, motivationally-based processes; physiological styles, biologically-based responses.

It is crucial to emphasize here that, practically speaking, not all the elements of learning style are of equal importance. Some of the styles have no generally acceptable testing techniques and others are still vague enough that much more investigation is needed. What is important at this point is that the reader understand the general concept of learning style and how the cognitive, affective, and physiological dimensions are related to it.

The following chart summarizes the major cognitive, affective, and physiological styles that have been discussed. Styles have been included because of the current significance of their research, their conceptual importance, or their practical utility. Many styles have been omitted either because their validity is uncertain, their application is questionable, or their meaning is subsumed in another style that is listed. A few conceptually debatable styles have been included only for their practical significance.

STUDENT LEARNING STYLE

Cognitive Styles

Reception Styles

Perceptual modality preferences
Field independence vs. dependence
Scanning
Constricted vs. flexible control
Tolerance for incongruous or
   unrealistic experiences
Strong vs. weak automatization
Conceptual vs. perceptual-motor
   dominance

Concept Formation and Retention Styles

Conceptual tempo
Conceptualizing styles
Breadth of categorizing
Cognitive complexity vs. simplicity
Leveling vs. sharpening

Affective Styles

Attention Styles

Conceptual level
Curiosity
Persistence or perseverance
Level of anxiety
Frustration tolerance

Expectancy and Incentive Styles

Locus of control
Achievement motivation
Self-actualization
Imitation
Risk taking vs. cautiousness
Competition vs. cooperation
Level of aspiration
Reaction to reinforcement
Social motivation
Personal interests

Physiological Styles

Sex-related behavior
Health-related behavior
Time-of-day rhythms
Need for mobility
Environmental elements

CHAPTER 2

Assessing Student Learning Style

FOR THOUSANDS OF YEARS, EDUCATORS HAVE sought to define education's role in meeting the needs of the individual. Socrates, in utilizing what is known today as the Socratic method, sought to foster individual development. Rousseau, in *Emile,* addressed the needs of the individual. John Dewey, in his monumental work at the beginning of the twentieth century, focused on the learner as an individual. In recent decades, considerable research and experimentation have been devoted to personalizing education.

Ultimately, education must come to grips with the different learning needs of individual learners. These learning differences flow from variations in individual intelligence, drive, skills, and accomplishment, as well as personal and family predispositions and the cultural influences of the wider society. In spite of considerable dialog, there is still substantial discontinuity between theory and practice in identifying and meeting these needs.

Today, some educators have intentionally departed from the traditional discussion of classroom materials and pupil-teacher ratios and are raising critical questions about the ways in which students learn. These efforts and related research focus on student learning skills and learning styles.

Much has been written about learning skills and we do not intend to treat this important issue at this time. Until recently, however, information and research on the ways that pupils learn have seldom been a part of proposals to personalize education. Yet, as society changes and costs increase, research on learning becomes increasingly significant. The key to effective schooling is to understand the range of student styles and to design instruction and materials that respond directly to individual learning needs.

The model of learning style outlined in Chapter 1 is helpful when thinking about the various instruments available for its assessment.

Learning styles are characteristic cognitive, affective, and physiological traits that serve as relatively stable indicators of how learners perceive, interact with, and respond to the learning environment. Current efforts to explain the underlying processes of learning and teaching reflect two lines of research. One group has dominant interest in the cognitive dimension of style. The other is concerned with applied models of learning and teaching and a multi-dimensional analysis of style.

Learning style analysis in school-based programs would seem to demand both approaches. Accordingly, we will review learning style assessment efforts under cognitive, affective, and physiological dimensions. We will cite examples of each of these domains and the types of psychometric measures that are available to assess them. Examples have been selected for their representativeness and diversity.

Cognitive Style Elements

Cognitive styles are "information processing habits representing the learner's typical mode of perceiving, thinking, problem solving, and remembering" (Messick et al., 1976). The vast majority of earlier research on personality-related learning variables dealt with cognitive style. Each learner has preferred ways of perception, organization, and retention that are distinctive and consistent. These characteristic differences are called cognitive styles.

The following styles and assessment devices illustrate the cognitive domain of learning style.

Perceptual modality preferences describe learner tendency to use the different sensory modes to understand experience. Perceptual response is both cognitive and affective in the sense that preferred response is a biased initial reaction to information. We prefer to get our information in ways that are pleasing to us. The conventional modes are kinesthetic or psychomotor, visual or spatial, and auditory or verbal. Orientation seems to evolve from kinesthetic to visual and eventually to verbal. All students ultimately need to learn to use all modalities with some effectiveness.

►The *Edmonds Learning Style Identification Exercise* (ELSIE) is a simple but effective method of detecting perceptual response. ELSIE is concerned with the ways students internalize individual words. It provides a profile of perceptual style based on the individual's pattern of response to 50 common English words that are read once at five-second intervals. Students are asked, upon hearing a word, to indicate which of the following responses occur to them most spontaneously:

1. *Visualization* — a mental picture of some object or activity
2. *Written Word* — a mental picture of the word spelled out
3. *Listening* — no mental picture but the sound of the word carries meaning
4. *Activity* — physical or emotional feeling about the word.

The learner's scores in all four categories are important. The profile is charted on a stanine scale arranged as bands above and below the median of a pilot group (See Reinert, 1976).

Field independence vs. dependence measures a continuum of an analytic as opposed to a non-analytic way of experiencing the environment. Independents see things apart from the background, but dependents are influenced by the overall organization of the background field and see parts of it as "fused." Independents differentiate among experiences while dependents see them as integrated. The field independent learner will tend to be highly analytic and systematic; the field dependent learner more holistic. This style has been the subject of much research.

▶The *Group Embedded Figures Test* (GEFT) is one of several embedded figures tests developed by Herman Witkin and his colleagues at Brooklyn College. The EFT was originally designed to assess cognitive functioning, social behavior, body concepts, etc. The group version of the test utilizes picture mazes (optical illusions) to assess analytical vs. nonanalytical styles of information processing. Test subjects are asked to identify and trace simple forms hidden within more complex figures. The following illustrates this technique. (The simple figure is located at the bottom right of the complex figure.)

Simple Form   Complex Figure

The GEFT is short and easy to administer. Widely used in research and, more recently, in classrooms, it actually measures level of analytical ability.

Bi-dimensional Models. A number of researchers have developed bi-dimensional models of cognitive style, combining two information processing dimensions. Anthony Gregorc's Style Delineator model, for example, looks at concrete vs. abstract and random vs. sequential styles. The resulting matrix profiles learners on four distinct learning patterns: Concrete Sequential (CS), Concrete Random (CR), Abstract Sequential (AS), and Abstract Random (AR).

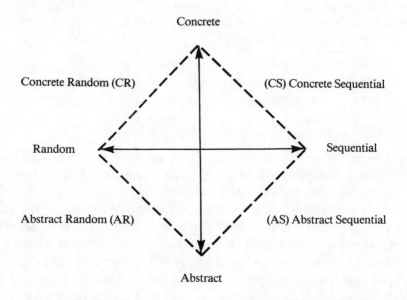

The Gregorc model has emerged from classroom research in diagnostic-prescriptive education as a means of exploring the match and mismatch implications of teaching and learning styles.

►The *Gregorc Style Delineator* assesses Gregorc's four bi-dimensional learning patterns. The inventory is a short, self-report instrument consisting of 40 words in 10 sets of 4 each. The student ranks personal impressions of the words in each set, identifying his or her spontaneous, natural ways of transacting with the learning environment. The resulting scores are visually profiled on a bi-dimensional matrix that shows the various style proclivities. Ninety percent of those tested have a definite preference in one or two of the four categories.

Cognitive Profiles — Charles Letteri of the University of Vermont has taken assessment of the information-processing domain a step further by combining several existing cognitive style elements in a profile that predicts student achievement on standardized achievement tests. This multi-dimensional Cognitive Profile charts the student's position across seven cognitive style continuums. Research projects dating back to 1977 have revealed three types of profiles:

- *Type I* is associated with high achievement levels in academic performance on standardized tests. This type of learner scores strongly on the majority of the following dimensions: analytical, focuser, narrow, complex, reflective, sharpener, and tolerant.
- *Type II* is descriptive of average performance on standardized tests and reflects an intermediate range on the style continuums, or a mixed profile — an inconsistent pattern of styles.
- *Type III* is characterized by low academic performance on standardized tests and by style proclivities in the majority of these dimensions: nonanalytical, nonfocuser, broad, simple, impulsive, leveler, intolerant.

No value judgments are implied in assigning these profiles, but they do assume a traditional school environment. Students in conventional settings with certain sets of characteristics score differently on standardized tests of school achievement. Letteri's "augmentation" research indicates that these style elements are trainable and that cognitive profiles can be altered. Schools that incorporate alternative learning environments may help to facilitate augmentation by providing conditions better suited to individual learners.

►The *Cognitive Profile* is derived from a battery of single bi-polar style tests that, in combination, predict student achievement on standardized tests. The test instruments are administered in their original clinical forms or in slightly modified versions. The styles and related continuums are listed below.

1. Field independence vs. field dependence — see above for definition.

       Analytical ◄——————————————————► Nonanalytical

2. Scanning — the degree of attention to task and susceptibility to distraction.

Focuser ◄───────────────► Nonfocuser

3. Breadth of categorization — the capacity to classify and organize tasks either in well-defined or in more general categories.

Narrow ◄───────────────► Broad

4. Cognitive complexity vs. simplicity — the different ways that persons construe the world and social behavior, ranging from a multi-dimensional to a uni-dimensional perspective.

Complex ◄───────────────► Simple

5. Reflectiveness vs. impulsivity — the consistency in the speed and accuracy of information gathering and hypothesis formation. Reflectives are slower and more accurate; impulsives faster and less accurate.

Reflective ◄───────────────► Impulsive

6. Leveling vs. sharpening — variations in memory processing. Sharpeners rely heavily on visual (rote) memory and recall data as distinct and different; levelers tend to blur memories and to confuse associated concepts.

Sharpener ◄───────────────► Leveler

7. Tolerance for incongruous or unrealistic experiences — differences in willingness to accept perceptions and experiences at variance with the conventional. Low tolerance implies a preference for more conventional ideas and approaches.

Tolerant ◄───────────────► Intolerant

Affective Style Elements

The second dimension of learning style encompasses personality traits that have to do with attention, emotion, and valuing — with the processes of motivation. Affective learning styles are the offshoots of motivation, viewed as the learner's typical mode of arousing, directing, and sustaining behavior.

Several characteristic affective styles and their supporting instrumentation are discussed in the following paragraphs.

Conceptual Level is a motivational trait developed by David Hunt at the Ontario Institute for the Study of Education. Conceptual Level (CL) describes the degree of structure a person needs to learn effectively. Low conceptual level signifies a need for high structure; high CL, that the learner needs less structure. Students typically develop through unsocialized, dependent, and independent stages, requiring successively less structure and showing increasing self-expression and autonomy.

►The *Paragraph Completion Method* (PCM) is a semi-projective method to assess Conceptual Level. Students are given six incomplete statements and are asked to write at least three sentences about each, telling how they really feel about the topic. The topics are:

1. What I think about rules . . .
2. When I am criticized . . .
3. What I think about parents . . .
4. When someone does not agree with me . . .
5. When I am not sure . . .
6. When I am told what to do . . .

The topics were chosen to reveal how students handle conflict. Completion responses are considered to be "thought samples" and are scored on a scale of 0-3 in terms of their conceptual complexity and developmental maturity. Scoring the PCM demands a cultivated clinical judgment based on training and practice.

Locus of Control is a construct that describes the forces within an individual's personality that direct or stimulate action. An individual's perceptions of causality may be internal or external. Internal individuals think of themselves as responsible for their own behavior. Externals see outer forces beyond their control as responsible for what happens. Internality is a highly desirable school-rated trait.

►The *I/E Scale* by Julian Rotter is one of several instruments available for the assessment of locus of control. The Rotter questionnaire presents a series of 29 paired alternatives that describe the ways certain important events in society affect different people. Test subjects are directed to select the one statement of each pair that they actually believe to be true. The statements present choices like the following:

a. Most of the problems in people's lives are a result of bad luck.
b. People's problems come from the mistakes they make.

The scale is quickly and easily hand scored.

Physiological Style Elements

The third domain of learning style includes the learning-related behaviors of the human body. Physiological styles are biologically based modes of response that are founded on sex-related differences, personal nutrition and health, and reaction to the physical environment.

Two elements illustrate the range of styles within this domain.

The *Environmental Elements* that influence learning are light, sound, and temperature. The related physiological learning styles are the individual learner's varying reactions to these elements. Few learners are bothered by minor lighting variations but many find it hard to work with even a small amount of noise. Temperature variations can be even more disturbing. Imagine the plight of the light-sensitive, shy, cold-blooded youngster who is forced to sit next to the window in a chilly, open-style classroom.

►No specialized instrument is available to measure environmental styles but the *Learning Style Inventory* (Dunn, Dunn, and Price) and the NASSP *Learning Style Profile* (Keefe and Monk) incorporate environmental elements as a major area of assessment. Teachers who are sensitive to the physiological implications of the learning environment can readily assess these elements by observation and provide options for students differently affected.

Time Rhythms are personal variations in learning readiness related to the time of day. Different persons learn better either in the morning, the afternoon, or at night. These differences likely reflect early childhood sleeping and waking patterns but may also derive from the more fundamental circadian rhythms of the body (the culprit in "jet lag").

►Rita and Kenneth Dunn have developed a simple *Time Questionnaire* to chart this element of style. The instrument is a short checklist that enables the learner to analyze preferred working times during the day. Scores are derived for early morning, late morning, afternoon, and evening. The questionnaire asks respondents to choose among such items as:

- I usually hate to get up in the morning.
- I usually feel a "low" after lunch.

The *Learning Style Inventory* and NASSP's *Learning Style Profile* both assess time-of-day preferences.

Comprehensive Instruments

A few researchers have formulated learning style instruments that assess more than one style dimension and several of the elements. Only the NASSP *Learning Style Profile* measures all major elements of the three dimensions of style. Other instruments primarily measure the cognitive and affective domains or the affective and physiological. Some examples follow.

COGNITIVE AND AFFECTIVE

►The Myers-Briggs Type Indicator (MBTI) is a measure of personality dispositions and preferences based on Carl Jung's theory of psychological "types." Jung postulated two basic bi-polar mental processes (sensing-intuition and thinking-feeling) and two fundamental orientations to life (extraversion and introversion). The MBTI adds a fourth dimension (judgment-perception) to identify the dominant mental process. The resulting matrix categorizes individuals into 16 types. The following diagram illustrates the relationships.

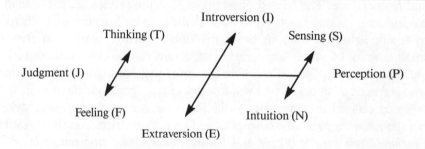

The MBTI provides information about the ways learners prefer to perceive meaning (sensing vs. intuition), to express values and commitment (sensing vs. feeling), and to interact with the world (extraversion and introversion). The judging vs. perceiving dimension simply identifies the learner's dominant preference in approaching reality (affective or cognitive).

The MBTI probably assesses personality orientation more than style. Typology is clearly broader than style so there may be some conceptual confusion in using the instrument for style alone. MBTI theory is sophisticated and the typology elaborate. Research is coordinated by the Center for Applications of Psychological Type (CAPT) in Gainesville, Florida.

▶*Cognitive Style Mapping* is the brain child of Joseph Hill, former president of Oakland Community College in East Lansing, Michigan. Hill developed mapping as a component of his conceptual framework for education which he called the "educational sciences." He expressed cognitive style in terms of mathematical set theory. In much simplified form, his framework would translate as follows:

5		1		2		3		4
Cognitive Style	=	Symbols and Meanings	×	Cultural Determinants	×	Modalities of Inference	×	Memory Functions

The fourth set — neurological, electrochemical, and biological aspects of memory functioning — has never been completed for lack of appropriate data.

The present theory and practice of cognitive style mapping is based on the interrelationship of the first three "sciences." Each of these dimensions is composed of various elements that interact to form an individual's cognitive style.

Symbols include words, names, sensory data, and psychomotor representations (games, sports, dance).

Cultural determinants are family and peer influences, and personal style preferences.

Modalities of influence are the inductive and deductive reasoning processes.

Two assessment techniques have been used in Cognitive Style Mapping.

1. Empirical Mapping uses systematic observation and the recording of information on the various style elements. It is ordinarily used with young children.
2. Mapping Inventories with statements keyed to the style elements have been developed at East Lansing (Michigan) High School; Ohio University in Athens, Ohio; and Mountain View Community College in Dallas, Texas. These instruments are self-report inventories that ask test

subjects to indicate whether they usually, sometimes, or rarely engage in the stated cognitive style behaviors.

The following are representative items.
- I prefer spoken directions instead of written ones.
- I can tell when someone is bluffing.
- I consult with my family before making decisions.
- I work best in an organized setting.

In some places, elaborate profiles are charted to represent each student's cognitive map.

Mapping presents an elegant theory of learning style and excellent item coverage of the perceptual, conceptualizing, and social motivation dimensions. Unfortunately, it suffers from a limited application in secondary schools and needs a current research base.

AFFECTIVE AND PHYSIOLOGICAL

The Learning Style Inventory (LSI) developed by Rita Dunn, Kenneth Dunn, and Gary Price is a widely used assessment instrument in elementary and secondary schools. The LSI incorporates many useful affective and physiological elements of learning style but only touches on the cognitive (in the area of perceptual modalities).

The Dunns and Price define learning style in terms of four pervasive learning conditions and 18 elements. Students complete a 104-item self-report questionnaire that identifies learning preferences about immediate environmental conditions and emotional, sociological, and physical needs. The inventory is designed to support alternative approaches to instruction by profiling the elements of each individual's learning style. The current version of the LSI assesses these 18 elements:

Environmental	*Emotional*	*Sociological*	*Physical*
Sound	Motivation	Self-oriented	Perceptual
Light	Persistence	Colleague-oriented	Intake
Temperature	Responsibility	Authority-oriented	Time
Design	Structure	Pair-oriented	Mobility
		Team-oriented	
		Varied	

Computerized scoring is available and provides individual and group profiles. Printouts show learning preferences on 22 subscales.

The Learning Style Inventory is a practitioner-oriented instrument with good reliability and widespread application, particularly in elementary and middle level schools. It lacks a definitive cognitive dimension, however, and several of the scales could benefit from better face and construct validation.

COGNITIVE, AFFECTIVE, AND PHYSIOLOGICAL

►The NASSP Learning Style Profile (LSP) is a second-generation instrument for the diagnosis of student cognitive styles, perceptual responses, study and instructional preferences. The Profile was developed by the NASSP research department (Keefe and Monk, 1986) in conjunction with a national task force of learning style experts. The task force spent almost a year reviewing the available literature and instrumentation before deciding to develop a new instrument.

The Profile was developed in four phases with initial work undertaken at the University of Vermont (cognitive elements), Ohio State University (affective elements), and St. John's University (physiological/environmental elements). Rigid validation and normative studies were conducted using factor analytic methods to ensure strong construct validity and subscale independence.

The Learning Style Profile contains 23 scales representing four higher order factors: cognitive styles, perceptual responses, study and instructional preferences (the affective and physiological elements). The LSP scales are as follows:

- Analytic Skill
- Spatial Skill
- Discrimination Skill
- Categorizing Skill
- Sequential Processing Skill
- Memory Skill
- Perceptual Response: Visual
- Perceptual Response: Auditory
- Perceptual Response: Emotive
- Persistence Orientation
- Verbal Risk Orientation
- Verbal-Spatial Preference
- Manipulative Preference
- Study Time Preference: Early Morning
- Study Time Preference: Late Morning
- Study Time Preference: Afternoon
- Study Time Preference: Evening
- Grouping Preference
- Posture Preference
- Mobility Preference
- Sound Preference
- Lighting Preference
- Temperature Preference

A Simultaneous Processing scale is still undergoing experimental testing and may be added to the Profile in the future.

The LSP is a first-level diagnostic tool intended to provide the basis for comprehensive style assessment. Extensive readability checks, reliability and validity studies, and factor analyses of the instrument, combined with the supervisory efforts of the task force, ensure valid use of the instrument with students in the sixth to twelfth grades. Computer scoring is available.

To further support diagnostic assessment, the task force is currently developing and field testing a computerized instructional management system that will enable teachers to more effectively relate instructional methodology to different student learning style profiles.

CHAPTER 3

Brain Behavior
and Learning Style

MUCH OF THE CURRENT LANGUAGE OF "whole-brain education" (and "right-brain education") is really metaphor for appropriate learning style analysis and flexible instructional application. The metaphor is sometimes misleading but the intent and often the outcomes are good. Systematic research on the brain is an important field of inquiry and major insights have been gained in recent years. Very little of what is known, however, has any direct implication for or application to education.

A great deal has been written in the literature of psychobiology and neurophysiology recently about the functions of the two hemispheres of the human brain. The beginnings of modern brain research, however, can be traced to the introduction of commissurotomy surgery in the 1940s and 1950s. In this operation, the connecting fibers — the *corpus callosum* is the largest — are severed between the right and left hemispheres of an epileptic or brain-damaged patient. Although most split-brain patients function very successfully after this operation, clinical testing reveals some interesting differences in their behavior.

Nobel Laureate Roger Sperry and his colleagues at the California Institute of Technology have worked for more than 20 years on split-brain research (e.g., Gazzaniga, Bogen, and Sperry, 1962). This research indicates that split-brain subjects respond to information in the right and left hemispheres very differently from brain-intact subjects. Each hemisphere of a split-brain subject is capable of perceiving, remembering, and responding, but often in its own characteristic way. The studies show that the left hemisphere is superior in verbal tasks incorporating phonics, syntax, or short-term memory, while the right is superior in visual-spatial tasks involving imagery, emotional tone, or the integration of experience. Similar research in visual perception (e.g., Barton, Goodglass, and Shai, 1965) and auditory perception (Kimura, 1961, 1967) suggests that these differential functions are also found in the hemispheres of the intact or normal brain.

Hemispheric Differences

Virtually every study of brain functioning supports the existence of hemispheric differences. Some researchers propose a speaking-nonspeaking or a verbal-nonverbal distinction. Others contend that the hemispheres basically differ in their approaches to processing, in the strategies they use to process information. Springer and Deutsch (1981) present an interesting list of the labels that have been applied to the differential functions of the brain. The listing is intended as a hierarchy with each subsequent label more inclusive than its antecedents.

Left Hemisphere	*Right Hemisphere*
Verbal	Nonverbal, visual-spatial
Sequential, temporal, digital	Simultaneous, spatial, analogic
Logical, analytic	Gestalt, synthetic
Rational	Intuitive
Western thought	Eastern thought

Most current researchers agree about the labels at the top of the list. The others are speculative. The verbal-nonverbal dichotomy is based on a large body of experimental research with both split-brain and normal subjects. The sequential-simultaneous distinction is a refinement of Luria's (1973) model of brain functioning. The analytic-holistic conceptualization comes from work of Jerre Levy (1974) and her colleagues that attempts to categorize the ways split-brain patients deal with incoming information.

SEQUENTIAL AND SIMULTANEOUS PROCESSING

The late Russian neuroscientist, A.R. Luria, developed a model of brain functioning based on 40 years of clinical work with persons who had suffered brain damage. Luria found that the brain works as a complete functioning system. His system includes three principal functional units:

1. A unit for regulating cortical tone in the outer layer of the cerebral hemispheres and cerebellum (the *arousal* unit)
2. A unit for obtaining, processing, and storing information from the external world (the *input* unit)
3. A unit for programming, regulating, and verifying mental activity (the *output/planning* unit for controlling the so-called executive functions).

Each of these three basic units is hierarchical in structure. Each has three cortical zones, from *primary* sensory and motor projection areas for receiving and sending impulses, to *secondary* associative ones where information is processed, to *tertiary* "zones of overlapping" for the most complex mental activities (Luria, 1973).

In 1979, Das, Kirby, and Jarman proposed a specific refinement of Luria's model to categorize his assessment tasks. They contend that simultaneous and successive processing are functions of the tertiary levels of Luria's units two and three. Sequential or successive processing is temporal, step-by-step ordering of experience. Speaking or computing are typical examples.

Simultaneous processing integrates the elements of experience without temporal ordering or stepwise relationships. Visual/spatial processing is the usual example. Some individuals can easily recognize other persons they have seen or met only briefly, but are not able to describe them, and vice versa. Individuals apply simultaneous and successive processing generically to all they experience.

Das, Kirby, and Jarman argue that simultaneous and successive processing are cognitive styles and related to other constructs such as field dependence-independence, reflectiveness-impulsivity, and conceptual level. They write:

> Cognitive styles can be conceived of as individual differences in preferred (or habitual) ways of processing information. As such, they will be intimately related to what we have termed Block 3 functions, the control and sequencing of cognitive operations in the solution of a task. . . . Subgroups can differ in their approaches to cognitive tasks, particularly with regard to the use of simultaneous and successive processing. From this perspective, simultaneous and successive processing can be seen as cognitive styles, or as ways of processing information. (Das, Kirby, and Jarman, 1979)

Investigations into the ways that the hemispheres of the brain process information led Levy (1974) to support an analytic vs. holistic distinction. The left hemisphere processes in a step-by-step fashion, breaking information into component parts and reorganizing it. Levy labeled this mode "analytic." The right hemisphere, by contrast, specializes in perceiving spatial patterns and relationships, which can be thought of as more holistic and synthetic. This conceptualization is somewhat more speculative than the sequential-simultaneous distinction but a logical extension of it.

The sequential-simultaneous distinction viewed as a cognitive style is probably the most meaningful application of current brain behavior research to instructional diagnosis and application. Indeed, these dimensions have been included in recent attempts to measure intelligence (Kaufman Assessment Battery for Children, 1983) and learning style (NASSP Learning Style Profile, 1986). The simultaneous and successive (sequential) processing dimensions provide an understandable link to brain function for learning style models that include cognitive modes (Languis, 1983). The analytic-holistic distinction adds little to the basic distinction of step-by-step vs. integrative modes of processing.

HEMISPHERIC MYTHOLOGY

Some researchers have tried to build a case for models of rational vs. intuitive processing or Western thought vs. Eastern thought. Ornstein (1972) in particular has championed the view that functions of the right hemisphere are neglected in Western societies. He associates rational, technological thinking with Western culture, and intuitive, mystical thinking with Eastern culture. The question comes down to whether these labels really represent distinct modes of thought or simply different strategies for processing information. The research seems to support the latter.

The seminal work on hemisphericity has led to a large amount of speculation on the subject. Hemispheric differences are purported to explain every conceivable kind of learning behavior from reading skill to artistic success. Ideas have evolved from the speaking-nonspeaking distinction to very complex notions that are more and more removed from basic research findings.

The term "dichotomania" has been used by some to describe the popular literature on the subject. This literature tends to equate the existence of hemispheric differences in the way the brain functions (research based) with actual hemispheric biases in learners (speculative). Individuals with good verbal skills are thought to use primarily their left hemispheres; those with good visual or spatial skills, primarily their right. The reality is that all learners use both hemispheres and both left and right hemispheric strategies in most of what they learn.

Neuropsychologists tell us that current naive notions of brain behavior are either false or lacking in any scientific validation. Yet many educators and educational writers accept them as true and even attempt to base educational practice on them. Levy (1982) puts the issue squarely in perspective.

> The realization that the whole brain is actively participating in perception, encoding of information, organization of representations, memory, arousal, planning, thinking, understanding, and all other mental operations whether it be a social interaction, painting a picture, playing the piano, doing mathematics, writing a story, attending a lecture, or seeing a movie, seems to have escaped many, if not most, popular writers.
>
> Only through misapprehension could some endeavors be attributed to left-hemisphere processes, and others to right-hemisphere processes. The two sides of the brain do differ, and they differ in quite important ways. The nature of these differences has little connection with the popularized picture, however, and the implications for human cognition and emotion are not what has been propagated.

Brain behavior research is still in its adolescence. Educational applications of this research are very much in their infancy. The truth is that very little application can be made in education of most of the research on hemispheric functioning. Some intriguing and highly speculative hypotheses abound. But very little can be verified.

Educators interested in carefully validated applications of brain behavior will have to wait a few years. Current attempts to tie brain functioning to instructional strategies are largely intuitive and anything but research-based, the claims of their proponents notwithstanding. Discussions about left-brain-biased schools and brain sensitive curricula are mostly guesswork and should be treated as speculative even if they are not particularly damaging. The most useful message this work brings to schools is that teaching should be flexible and responsive to learner processing preferences.

Whole Brain Education

Successful education is "whole-brain education." Students surely do *not* learn with only one hemisphere of the brain but they do respond to information differently. Some individuals, for example, show a preference or a selective attention to the left or right visual fields. Those with a leftward bias favor the right hemisphere and do better on face-recognition tasks; those with a rightward bias favor the left hemisphere and do better on phonetic analysis (Levy, 1982). Students with these biases may learn certain tasks better with either visual or verbal methods. But whether the learner shows a preference for one or the other processing strategies, the *whole* brain processes the information.

The issue here is one of hemispheric "dominance," the tendency of one hemisphere to take over processing and to control in responding to incoming information. Generally, the hemisphere with a greater capacity for a task (verbal or spatial) will tend to dominate. But Levy and Trevarthen (1976) found in "chimeric figure" tests (split-composite faces) that the anticipated response did not always occur. Sometimes the expected hemisphere responded with the unexpected process or the unexpected hemisphere with the expected one.

In general, hemispheric differences seem to be relative rather than absolute. Either hemisphere can probably function in either mode of processing, depending partly on the nature of the task and partly on the experience and preference of the learner. Levy and Trevarthen (1976) speculates that "hemispheric activation does not depend on a hemisphere's real aptitude or even on its actual processing strategy on a given occasion, but rather on what it *thinks* it can do." Hemispheric dominance may be as much a matter of preference as any innate predisposition. Students learn better with different methods because they prefer certain processing patterns. Some learners, for example, prefer verbal activities and others, visual-spatial activities in learning basic skills tasks. But the more complicated the task, the more "whole-brained" the response will be in all learners.

Learning style analysis provides some insight into individual differences in preference and predisposition. Whole-brain learning requires systematic diagnosis of learner processing strengths and weaknesses, and appropriate use of instructional strategies and methods. Regrettably, the research linking brain function with all these processes has not yet been done. Working models are available and the experience of a few successful programs. Yet, some useful school applications can be made while the research continues.

CHAPTER 4

Applications of Learning Style

FOR MORE THAN A CENTURY, EDUCATORS have been searching for solutions to what may be educations's most basic dilemma: What should schools do about individual differences among learners?

In the past, educators viewed learning as a commodity stored in the minds of teachers and waiting to be dispensed. The responsibility of teachers was to impart; that of students, to partake. If students did not learn, the fault was theirs. Teachers were not expected to adjust to the inability of students to learn the way they taught. If the student could not adapt, the fault was the student's.

Nineteenth century educators were very much influenced by Darwinist thought. Social mobility was open to anyone who could compete for more education. Competition was the reigning ethic. Early Social Darwinists following Spencer preached competition and merit rather than hereditary privilege as the basis for preferment.

Ward and other later Social Darwinists began to emphasize the need to modify the environment. The turn of the century "scientific movement in education" looked for answers to such questions as "When should children begin school?" or "What is the *best* method of teaching reading?" Educators turned their attention to modifying the learning environment, but in one direction — toward a standard way of doing things. Standardization became the primary concern of schooling.

The progressive movement attempted to confront the problems of standardization. Progressivists broadened their inquiries beyond "best" solutions to look at varying student aptitudes and learning environments. The question became, "How can we improve instruction to meet the needs of different learners?" Reform movements came and passed; but hardly a ripple remained. And generally, no one had any regrets. Most of the attempts seemed faddish — the ebbs and tides of the school mainstream.

Even the great innovative surge of the 1960s was disappointing. Innovators of that decade felt secure in the conviction that every human being was unique. Accordingly, schools had to be designed for students, not for administrative convenience. Then came the financial crunch of the 1970s and test score declines. Some programs had to be cut back and others strengthened. Apparently, once again, the efforts at improvement had been faulty; otherwise, why would test scores decline? It was time to rethink the premise.

Like most scenarios, this one has its measure of fact and fiction. Test scores declined for many reasons, chief among them that schools had moved their emphasis from building on basic skills to "providing alternatives." The baby had often been thrown out with the bathwater. It was certainly time to reestablish a solid foundation of reading, writing, and math skills before aspiring to more sophisticated goals. But, at the same time, even if the new programs had failed, it was not that the concepts were flawed, but that they had not been adequately tried.

John Goodlad (1970) in his famous *Look Behind the Classroom Door* found that most innovations were honored in the breach rather than in the observance. Contemporary schools were long on good intentions and short on instructional strategy. Even the best of the new programs were disappointing because single-minded traditional techniques had been traded for single-minded innovative ones. The reality of individual differences demanded approaches founded on the fact of diversity. What was needed was more variety for some students and less for others; structured programs for dependent learners and options for independent ones.

The goal of personalizing learning and instruction is an historical one. It is a quest that may now be within our grasp with the emergence of new diagnostic and instructional techniques. Previous efforts were unsuccessful because they were based on a false epistemology, on a misunderstanding of how students learn.

Is it any wonder that school reform has faltered when we consider the dearth of practitioner knowledge about learning, the reliance largely on learner or parental preference in student scheduling rather than on careful diagnosis of needs, the futile attempts to make all students learn by the same methods, new or old? Now, however, we have the beginnings of a science of human learning that can be applied in schools.

The concept of learning style revives the hope for authentic personalized education since it starts with the learner and then proceeds logically to a consideration of the teaching and learning environment. An understanding of the ways students learn is the door to educational improvement. And learning style diagnosis is the key to an understanding of student learning.

Views of Style

Today, style researchers and practitioners generally fall into two schools of thought.

1. Cognitive researchers and theorists continue to examine different instructional variables and conditions in search of basic teaching and learning models.

Some contemporary cognitive scientists, for example, argue against individualizing instructional settings and for helping learners cope with the *existing* learning environment. These researchers accept the premise that some cognitive styles are more productive of school achievement than others. They build on the skills the learner already has and train the more adaptive skills for transfer to other school learning situations. If, for example, a student has difficulty in problem-solving tasks, cognitive proponents would train for greater problem-solving skills.

2. Practitioners and some researchers concentrate on various innovative ways of changing the teaching/learning environment to accommodate the needs of different types of learners.

Proponents of individualization, for example, believe in modifying the learning environment, not training the child. Hypothesizing that student learning style and cognitive skills are relatively stable, these practitioners and researchers advocate wide variety in learning settings, resources, and instructional methodologies. If a student has difficulty in problem-solving tasks, they would modify the instructional setting.

Middle ground does exist. The cognitive development theory of Jean Piaget offers a sound philosophical position for reconciling the opposing views.

Piaget's approach to human behavior and learning reflects his formal training in the biological sciences. In nature, species adapt both to meet the demands and to utilize the resources of the environment. Piaget uses two principles of biological evolution in his theory of cognitive development.

1. *New structures develop in nature to fill old functions under changed conditions;* e.g., the human ear evolved from one of the gill arches of fish. Development always is rooted in what exists and shows continuity with the past. Piaget applies this principle to human behavior at each age by showing how learning structures adapt to the environment and to one another, and allow the learner to modify the environment in return. When a child begins to talk, he is able to achieve things he could not do before and also to set new goals. The student who improves task analysis skills can tackle ordinary learning more effectively and reach out to more difficult projects.

2. *Adaptations in nature develop, not in isolation, but congruously within the total environment;* e.g., marsupials evolved in Australia to fill the same ecological niches that mammals occupy on other continents. Human adaptation is a function not only of man's nature but of the total system in which he functions. For example, the pervasive influence of speech in human culture is evident in all our structures and social conventions. Human society is organized for verbal communication. That learning assumes verbal communication influences the way we organize classrooms, invent technology, and group learners for instruction.

Piaget views intelligence as a specific instance of *adaptive* behavior, the ability to organize and cope with the experiences of the environment.

Assimilation and *accommodation* are the complementary processes of *adaptation*. In assimilation, the learner takes in sensations or experiences without having to modify existing processing structures. He handles new problems and circumstances with the present stock of experiences (schemas), interpreting new situations in terms of old ones, and reacting as in past situations.

In accommodation, the learner *modifies* existing schemas to adapt to the demands of the external environment. He accommodates to the unfamiliar environment by changing behavior. Through accommodation, individuals respond to situations that are initially too demanding, for which past responses are no longer adequate.

The balance ("equilibration") between the process of assimilation and accommodation is called adaptation. Piaget views the individual and the environment as a gestalt. The student and teacher not only act and react singly but the system behaves as a whole. The learner is both contributor to and recipient of the learning process.

Several authors (Hunt, 1971; Ginsburg and Opper, 1979; Weil and Murphy, 1982) suggest that adaptive growth takes place when the challenge in the learning environment is different enough from what is already mastered to motivate attempts at modifying the individual's cognitive structure.

In Piagetian terms, again, learning depends on an appropriate discrepancy between the learner's assimilative and accommodative capacities and the difficulty of the task. Weil and Murphy (1982) see teachers acting as facilitators of cognitive conflict and restructuring. From this perspective, instruction is effective to the degree that it creates an appropriate imbalance between the individual and the environment, and a new equilibrium that is more stable and responsive than before. The constant readjustment inherent in the process constitutes mental development (Inhelder and Piaget, 1958).

Cognitive growth, then, can come from adapting the environment to the existing skills of the learner (assimilation), or from helping the individual adapt successfully to the demands of the environment (accommodation). These bi-polar approaches can be thought of as a program-person continuum of learning strategies.

Learning Intervention Strategies

Program ◄————————————► Person

Depending on the individual's age, developmental capacities, and skill levels, both remediation of cognitive skills and personalization of the learning environment can be appropriate adaptive behaviors.

Personalized Education

The inputs to teaching and learning largely determine what the outcomes will be. Let us turn briefly to a model of education that is concerned with an *adaptive* view of the process.

No educational program can be successful without attention to the personal learning needs of individual students. A single approach to instruction, whether traditional or innovative, simply does not do the job. Contemporary research on learner and teacher traits is building a conceptual base for change in instructional practice. This research gives support to the concepts of personalized or adaptive education — to a teaching/ learning cycle of diagnosis, prescription, instruction, and evaluation (DPIE).

All learning is entirely personal. Readiness and incentive, style and rate of learning, preferred methodology and content, all vary widely from person to person. A personalized view of education accepts students where they are and establishes an adaptive instructional environment, one in which a student can gain success through effort.

Personalized education is a systematic effort on the part of a school to take into account individual student characteristics and effective instructional practices in organizing the learning environment. Carroll (1975) calls it "an attempt to achieve a balance between the characteristics of the learner and the learning environment." It is a match of the learning environment with the learner's knowledge, processing strategies, concepts, learning sets, motivational systems, and acquired skills. And it is a continual process.

Ideally, personalization tailors the teaching-learning process to the individual. In practice, it takes many forms depending on the available human and instructional resources. No one way of personalizing education is best.

Personalized education begins with learner needs and utilizes skills training and adaptive instructional strategies to build the learning environment. It is characterized by comprehensive diagnosis of student entry characteristics, careful student-teacher-parent planning, flexible program placement, and state-of-the-art instruction and evaluation. Above all, it uses careful diagnostic assessment, a component that is missing or incomplete in most of its forerunners. The figure presents an applied model of personalized education.

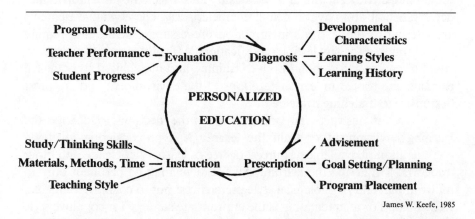

James W. Keefe, 1985

1. Diagnosis is concerned with student traits, learning problems, and the nature of the learning environment. It encompasses student developmental characteristics, learning history (Bloom's term for acquired knowledge and skills), and learning style. Learning style is a key element of diagnosis.
2. Prescription includes advisement, goal setting, program planning, and placement. Teachers determine appropriate instructional objectives and activities, recommend grouping and scheduling alternatives, and serve

as teacher advisers to a small number of students.
3. Adaptive Instruction is concerned with teaching styles and methodologies, student learning skills, and time use. Teachers structure the learning environment, train students in study and thinking skills, and manage time use, etc.
4. Evaluation includes appropriate student assessment, teacher supervision, administrator growth profiling, and program evaluation.

Feedback from this entire evaluative process is the basis for: a) continuation, modification, or termination of a given program, b) continuing diagnosis of student needs, and c) repetition of the entire diagnostic-prescriptive cycle.

Significance of the Style Concept

The NASSP Learning Styles Task Force defined learning style as "the composite of characteristic cognitive, affective, and physiological factors that serve as relatively stable indicators of how a learner perceives, interacts with, and responds to the learning environment. It is demonstrated in that pattern of behavior and performance by which an individual approaches educational experiences. Its basis lies in the structure of neural organization and personality that both molds and is molded by human development and the learning experiences of home, school, and society." (Keefe and Languis, 1983)

Learning style has cognitive, motivational, and behavioral elements rooted in genetic structure and personality and affected by the individual's developmental and environmental characteristics. The cognitive elements are internal to the learner's information processing structure and require careful training for any lasting modification. Affective elements are preferential in nature and respond both to training and matching. Physiological elements are rooted in learner reactions to the environment and are most responsive to matching strategies.

From an instructional point of view, the decision to change the learning environment or train the learner is a practical one involving consideration of available resources, degree of learner deficiency, and other tradeoffs. Modifying the learning environment may be pertinent only to motivational and physiological style preferences, not to cognitive elements. Remediation or augmentation is the appropriate strategy for cognitive style "growth"; personalization, for affective and physiological style "match."

Learning style diagnosis in all probability offers the most useful answer to our opening question, "What should schools do about individual differences among learners?" If we wish students to have optimum learning experiences in our schools, we must change the ways we deliver instruction.

Some learners clearly need more responsive instructional environments. (Most recent innovative teaching methods reflect this point of view.) Other learners need better cognitive skills to cope with the existing learning environment. If a youngster fails to respond even to matched conditions of learning, then we must retrain his or her cognitive styles to make school success possible. Indeed, some learners require both cognitive training and more personalized programs of instruction to achieve success in school.

Schoolwide Implementation

In our introductory chapter, we explored 32 cognitive, affective, and physiological learning styles. The listing, of course, is tentative and lengthy. The fact is that learning style is only now beginning to emerge from the laboratory and field-testing stages. To the practitioner, the view may still be obscure.

The question arises: What should the school staff do to systematically identify individual student learning styles? A number of alternatives are possible depending on the extent of a school's commitment to style assessment and structural change.

1. *A remedial approach.* Single out one or two learning styles that have readily available testing instrumentation and proceed in therapeutic fashion. Administer the test or inventory to those students who seem to have difficulty with the school's dominant learning environment (e.g., traditional, core, tracked, etc.). Look for general trends; i.e., whether most of the students having trouble exhibit similar learning profiles.

A school opting for this approach might want to use one or two of the simpler assessment techniques such as the *Group Embedded Figures Test* by Witkin (field independence/dependence) or the *Edmonds Learning Style Identification Exercise* by Reinert (perceptual preferences). Students assessed as less analytic could be trained in problem-solving skills and provided with more holistic instruction. Students with widely varying perceptual preferences could be accommodated.

2. *A diagnostic approach.* Select one of the comprehensive instruments such as the NASSP Learning Style Profile to identify the learning skills and preferences of all students in the entering class of the school (e.g., grades 6 or 7, 9 or 10). Test the transfer students. Then use the diagnostic data for student placement, goal setting, and appropriate counseling.

More knowledge and commitment are necessary at this level of implementation. One or more school staff members must become experts in learning style analysis. Staff inservice will ultimately determine the success of the effort. Good sources of additional information are the references at the end of this book, contact with pioneering schools already implementing learning style programs, and inservice activities such as the NASSP Learning Style Profile Workshops and Training Seminars.

3. *Organizing the entire school for personalization.* Utilize one or more of the assessment techniques above and involve the entire staff in diagnosis, prescription, and evaluation. Enlist teachers and others as student advisers to assist in the diagnostic function. Staff development will be even more important in this kind of all-out effort. And there must be adequate time in the schedule and sufficient administrative support to make real diagnosis

and advisement possible. Schools may need the services of specially trained *cognitive resource teachers* to support this level of implementation.

Significant attention to the diagnostic and planning functions of personalization will significantly change the role of the guidance counselor. School counselors will be called upon to do more educational counseling. They will rejoin the instructional team in a new role by preparing teachers for the diagnostic function. Where a system of teacher advisers already exists, advisers and counselors will play a more powerful role in the diagnostic process.

A school that adopts this approach acknowledges, at least implicitly, the validity of our personalized education model. The only solid foundation for a responsive learning environment is careful diagnosis of individual learner traits followed by flexible instruction and systematic evaluation. Learning is not a one-way process but an interactive one.

Classroom Applications

When school organization cannot support a more comprehensive approach, classroom teachers can still diagnose certain dimensions of learning style and modify instruction to accommodate individual differences. If no special testing budget is available, teachers can begin by observing students and answering a few diagnostic questions. The following examples are based on the elements of perceptual modality, conceptual tempo, concept formation, and on motivational and physiological styles.[1]

Perceptual Modality

People perceive reality in three basic ways: through the visual (reading and viewing), the aural (hearing and speaking), and the psychomotor (doing). Perceptual preference seems to evolve for most students from psychomotor to visual and aural as the learner matures. A dominant preference usually forms early in life, however, and does not change radically.

We are not suggesting that perceptual style is a matter of student choice, but that preference develops from infancy almost subconsciously. A teacher alert to these preferences can arrange for flexibility in grouping, materials, and teaching style.

To assess dominant perceptual modality, the teacher can ask the following kinds of questions:

- What kinds of learning activities does the learner seem to need? Handle the best?

---

1. The material is based, in part, on "Individual Differences in Learning Styles" by A. Shumsky and "Learning Performance and Individual Differences: Prospective" by L. Sperry. In *Learning Performance and Individual Differences,* edited by L. Sperry (Glenview, Ill.: Scott, Foresman and Company, 1972.)

- What kinds of activities do *not* hold his attention?
- Does he remember better if he reads silently, reads and listens, listens only, or engages in an activity?
- Are his word associations and speech patterns more visual (uses of imagery), aural (verbally articulate), or behavioral (action-oriented)?

Conceptual Tempo

Learners differ in the amount of time they need to get down to work and to complete a learning task. They tend to work slowly with precision or quickly with abandon. In terms of tempo, people are more or less reflective, more or less impulsive.

Schools interested in optimizing student time-on-task should provide for pacing alternatives. Students who need a great deal of structure to work successfully should have close supervision and few distractions. Reflective students can be given much more flexibility to use resources in the community, to develop exploratory experiences, etc.

Teachers also will want to analyze their personal conceptual tempos in order to know how they affect their students' learning rates. Yando and Kagan (1968) found that reflective teachers foster reflectiveness but impulsive teachers have little impact on students' tempo. Sperry (1972) suggests some interesting implications of this phenomenon:

> A teacher with a reflective tempo is likely to associate quickness with intelligence and will tend to reward impulsive learners who rapidly and accurately respond. The less able impulsive learner will then be at a disadvantage if speed of response is associated with inaccuracies in responding. This learner is being taught to value quickness, yet quickness may only enhance the learner's likelihood of failure.

Teachers can ask themselves these questions to diagnose conceptual tempo:

- Does the student work deliberately and accurately, or quickly and inaccurately?
- Does he work at the same pace for all tasks or vary his rate depending on the level of challenge?
- Does he aim to do good work or just finish an assignment?

Concept Formation

Some students grasp abstract concepts readily while others need concrete imagery to learn. Some use a broad, holistic approach to problem solving while others proceed small step by small step. Some learners are more analytic than others. One of the reasons that inductive, discovery-oriented approaches have not worked as a general methodology is that inquiry is most appropriate for the analytic learner. A lecture approach is better suited to the non-analytic type.

A teacher attempting to assess problem-solving preferences should determine:

- Does the learner see the world as complex or generally uncomplicated?
- Is he able to grasp the central idea of an issue or problem? Use information in new and different ways?
- Does he tend to define things abstractly or in concrete terms?
- Does he try to see the "big picture" before attempting a learning task, or does he begin immediately, working in a narrow, linear fashion?

Motivational Factors

Affective learning styles are a by-product of learner personality, cultural environment, parental and peer pressures, and school influences. Students are motivated or not by the school itself, their teachers, and the subjects they study. They are influenced by their general level of curiosity, need for structure, desire for excellence, and simple personal interests. Indeed, knowing one's own learning style can be motivational in itself.

We do not know, conclusively, which elements of motivation are most significant for school learning, but research by Chiu Lian-Hwang (1967) has distinguished five relatively independent factors. The teacher will want to ask questions based on these factors to derive a motivational profile:

- Does the student have a positive orientation toward learning? Does he show persistence and a high level of aspiration? Does he have positive feelings toward his academic self-concept and past performance?
- Does he manifest a need for academic recognition from teachers and peers?
- Does he fear failure and try to avoid it to a reasonable degree? (Underachievers may be too anxious or too bored to learn well.)
- Is he curious, both about concepts and about things?
- Does he work when the teacher demands it, or his parents, or even his friends? Is he responsive to authority and peer influence?

Physiological Factors

The physical and environmental have more influence on the learning process than most teachers and administrators acknowledge. The way a student feels, whether he has had a nourishing breakfast, the time of day, the layout and atmosphere of the classroom, all these elements affect student performance. Teachers sensitive to the physiological influences on learning can provide a learning environment with useful options, and learn to adapt classroom activities to individual differences.

Fortunately, physiological styles lend themselves readily to assessment by observation and simple questions. Teachers can ask themselves and their students:

- Does this student seem to get adequate nourishment at home and at school to work efficiently? Is his health reasonably good? Is he performing to the level of his physical abilities?
- Is he a morning or afternoon person? Is he able to function adequately

during his "down time"?

- Can he sit still during the more demanding learning activities or is he inclined to fidget? Does he want to wander around?
- Does he require average or higher levels of lighting?
- Does noise (or music) seem to bother or help him?
- Are any of the males frustrated by the type and level of verbal tasks required? Do any of the females balk at laboratory activities or other visual-spatial tasks?

Concluding Suggestions

Learning style is much more than another innovation. It is a fundamental new tool for teachers and students. It is a new way of looking at learning and instruction, providing a deeper and more profound view of the learner than known previously. It is a basic framework upon which a theory and practice of instruction can be built. It makes obsolete any single framework for teaching all students. All recent developments in instructional strategy and methodology must be rethought in the light of learning style.

It is nothing less than revolutionary to base instructional planning on an analysis of each student's learning characteristics. To do so moves education away from the traditional assembly-line, mass production model to a handcrafted one. It also means, perhaps for the first time, that educators have more to work with than just conventional wisdom about students and learning.

A practical perspective would be to take an easy first step, either schoolwide or within individual classrooms. Patricia Cross (1976) and others propose some possibilities:

1. Establish a systematic program of inservice on learning styles for teachers, students, and parents.
2. Arrange for an interested teacher or administrator to receive special training in learning/cognitive style analysis and augmentation (remediation). Cognitive resource teachers will soon be as important to a school as reading specialists.
3. Work toward a more flexible learning environment in the school. No method of instruction works for all students. Provide alternatives. Avoid systematically biasing instruction in favor of any one learning style.
4. Make certain that basic skills instruction reflects some systematic form of student learning styles diagnosis.
5. Concentrate on better student advisement and guidance. The learning style concept is relatively value-fair and has great potential for improving academic program planning and career counseling.
6. Keep an open mind. Much is known already about learning styles. The research is growing rapidly. Effective new instrumentation like the NASSP Learning Style Profile makes assessment more convenient and doable. Many schools have accomplished a great deal;

others must take up the challenge.

Educators must learn to base programs on the significant differences that exist among learners rather than on the assumption that everybody learns in the same way. Learning style accepts individual differences as normative and views them as a challenge rather than a liability.

Learning style diagnosis opens the door to personalizing education on a rational basis. It gives the most powerful leverage yet available to educators to analyze, motivate, and assist students in school. It is the foundation of a truly modern approach to education.

References

Allen, M. "Models of Hemispheric Specialization." *Psychological Bulletin* 1(1983):73-104.

Alpert, R., and Haber, R.N. "Anxiety in Academic Achievement Settings." *Journal of Abnormal and Social Psychology* 61(1960):207-15.

Alschuler, A.S. *Developing Achievement Motivation in Adolescents.* Englewood Cliffs, N.J.: Educational Technology Publications, 1973.

Bachman, J.G. "Motivation in a Task Situation as a Function of Ability and Control Over Task." *Journal of Abnormal and Social Psychology* 69(1964):272-81.

Baldwin, A.L. *Theories of Child Development.* New York: John Wiley and Sons, 1967.

Ball, S., ed. *Motivation in Education.* New York: Academic Press, 1977.

Bandura, A. "Social Learning Through Imitation." In *Nebraska Symposium on Motivation: 1962,* edited by M.R. Jones. Lincoln, Nebr.: University of Nebraska Press, 1962.

Barton, M.I.; Goodglass, H.; and Shai, A. "The Differential Recognition of Tachistoscopically Presented English and Hebrew Words in the Right and Left Visual Fields." *Perceptual and Motor Skills* 21(1965):431-47.

Berlyne, D.E. "A Theory of Human Curiosity." *British Journal of Psychology* 45(1954):180-91.

Bieri, J. "Complexity-Simplicity as a Personality Variable in Cognitive and Preferential Behavior." In *Functions of Varied Experience,* edited by D.W. Fiske and S.R. Maddi. Homewood, Ill.: Dorsey Press, 1961.

Bloom, B.S. *Human Characteristics and School Learning.* New York: McGraw-Hill, 1976.

Bradshaw, J.L., and Nettleton, N.C. "The Nature of Hemispheric Specialization in Man." *The Behavioral and Brain Sciences* 4(1981):51-91.

Brookover, W.B.; Shailer, T.; and Paterson, A. "Self-Concept of Ability and School Achievement." *Sociology of Education* 37(1964).

Broverman, D.M. "Cognitive Style and Intra-Individual Variations in Abilities." *Journal of Personality* 28(1960a):240-56.

_____. "Dimensions of Cognitive Style." *Journal of Personality* 28(1960b):167-85.

Bruner, J.S.; Oliver, R.R.; and Greenfield, P.M. *Studies in Cognitive Growth.* New York: Wiley, 1966.

Bryden, M.P. *Laterality: Functional Asymmetry in the Intact Brain.* New York: Harcourt Brace Jovanovich, 1982.

Carroll, A.W. *Personalizing Education in the Classroom.* Denver, Colo.: Love Publishing Co., 1975.

Carroll, J.B. "A Model of School Learning." *Teachers College Record*

64(1963):723-33.

Chall, J.S., and Mersky, A.F., eds. *Education and the Brain*. Seventy-seventh Yearbook of the National Society for the Study of Education, Part II. Chicago: University of Chicago Press, 1978.

Chiu, L.H. "A Factorial Study of Academic Motivation." Doctoral dissertation, Teachers College, Columbia University, 1967.

Crandall, V.; Katkovsky, W.; and Crandall, V. "Children's Beliefs in Their Own Control of Reinforcements in Intellectual-Academic Situations." *Child Development* 36(1965):91-109.

Cravioto, J. "The Effect of Malnutrition on the Individual." Paper presented at the International Conference on Nutrition, National Development, and Planning, Massachusetts Institute of Technology, Cambridge, Mass., 1971.

Cronbach, L.J., and Snow, R.E. *Aptitudes and Instructional Methods*. New York: Irvington Publishers, 1977.

Cross, K.P. *Accent on Learning*. San Francisco: Jossey-Bass, 1976.

Das, J.P.; Kirby, J.R.; and Jarman, F.F. *Simultaneous and Successive Processes*. New York: Academic Press, 1979.

Davis, J. *Technical Report #32: Concept Identification as a Function of Cognitive Style, Complexity, and Training Procedure*. Madison, Wis.: Center for Cognitive Learning, 1967.

Dermer, M., and Berscheid, E. "Self-Report of Arousal as an Indicant of Activation Level." *Behavioral Science* 17(1972):420-29.

Deutsch, M. "The Effects of Cooperation and Competition on Group Process." In *Group Dynamics: Research and Theory*, edited by D. Cartwright and A. Zander. Evanston, Ill.: Row and Peterson, 1960.

Dunn, R., and Dunn, K. *Teaching Students Through Their Individual Learning Styles*. Reston, Va.: Reston Publishing, 1978.

Fitt, S. "The Individual and His Environment." In *Learning Environments*, edited by T.G. David and B.D. Wright. Chicago: University of Chicago Press, 1975.

Gardner, R.W., and Long, R.I. "Control Defense and Concentration Effort: A Study of Scanning Behavior." *British Journal of Psychology* 53(1962):129-40.

Gardner, R.W.; Holzman, P.S.; Klein, G.S.; Linton, H.B.; and Spence, D.P. "Cognitive Control: A Study of Individual Consistencies in Cognitive Behavior." *Psychological Issues* 1(1959):4.

Gazzaniga, M.S.; Bogen, J.E.; and Sperry, R.W. "Some Functional Effects of Sectioning the Cerebral Commissures in Man." *Proceedings of the National Academy of Sciences* 48(1962):1765.

Ginsburg, H., and Opper, S. *Piaget's Theory of Intellectual Development*, 2nd ed. Englewood Cliffs, N.J.: Prentice-Hall, 1979.

Goodlad, J.I.; Klein, M.F.; and Associates. *Behind the Classroom Door*. Worthington, Ohio: Charles A. Jones, 1970.

Gregorc, A.F. "Learning/Teaching Styles: Potent Forces Behind Them." *Educational Leadership* 36(1979):234-36.

———. *An Adult's Guide to Style*. Maynard, Mass.: Gabriel Systems,

1982.

Hawkins, G. "Motivation and Individual Learning Styles." *Engineering Education* 65(1974):407-11.

Hill, J.E. *The Educational Sciences,* rev. ed. Bloomfield Hills, Mich.: Oakland Community College, 1976.

Hill, J.E., et al. *Personalizing Educational Programs Utilizing Cognitive Style Mapping.* Bloomfield Hills, Mich.: Oakland Community College, 1971.

Hines, T.M. "Neuroscience." In *Encyclopedia of Educational Research,* 5th ed., edited by H.E. Mitzel. New York: The Free Press, 1982.

Holzman, P.S. "Scanning: A Principle of Reality Contact." *Perceptual and Motor Skills* 23(1966):835-44.

Holzman, P.S., and Gardner, R.W. "Leveling-Sharpening and Memory Organization." *Journal of Abnormal and Social Psychology* 61(1960):176-80.

Holzman, P.S., and Klein, G.S. "Cognitive System — Principles of Leveling and Sharpening: Individual Differences in Assimilation Effects in Visual Time Error." *Journal of Psychology* 37(1954):105-22.

Hunt, D.E. *Matching Models in Education.* Toronto: Ontario Institute for Studies in Education, 1971.

Hunt, D.E.; Butler, L.F.; Noy, J.E.; and Rosser, M.E. *Assessing Conceptual Level by the Paragraph Completion Method.* Toronto: Ontario Institute for Studies in Education, 1978.

Inhelder, B., and Piaget, J. *The Growth of Logical Thinking from Childhood to Adolescence.* New York: Basic Books, 1958.

Joyce, B., and Weil, M. *Models of Teaching,* 2nd ed. Englewood Cliffs, N.J.: Prentice-Hall, Inc., 1979.

Kagan, J. "The Concept of Identification." *Psychological Review* 65(1958):296-305.

_____."Reflection-Impulsivity: The Generality and Dynamics of Conceptual Tempo." *Journal of Abnormal Psychology* 71(1966):17-24.

Kagan, J., and Wright, J. *Basic Cognitive Processes in Children.* Lafayette, Ind.: Child Development Publications, 1963.

Kagan, J.; Moss, H.A.; and Sigel, I.E. "Psychological Significance of Styles of Conceptualization." *Monographs of the Society for Research in Child Development* 28(1963):73-112.

Kaufman, A.S., and Kaufman, N.L. *Kaufman Assessment Battery for Children.* Circle Pines, Minn.: American Guidance Service, 1983.

Keefe, J.W. "Personalized Education." In *Instructional Leadership Handbook,* edited by J.W. Keefe and J.M. Jenkins. Reston, Va.: NASSP, 1984.

_____."Assessment of Learning Styles Variables: The NASSP Task Force Model." *Theory Into Practice,* Spring 1985, pp.138-44.

Keefe, J.W., and Languis, M.L. "Operational Definitions." Paper presented to the NASSP Learning Styles Task Force, Reston, Va. 1983.

Keefe, J.W., and Monk, J.S. *Learning Style Profile Examiner's Manual.* Reston, Va.: NASSP, 1986.

Kimura, D. "Cerebral Dominance and the Perception of Verbal Stimuli." *Canadian Journal of Psychology* 15(1961):166-71.

_____. "Functional Asymmetry of the Brain in Dichotic Listening." *Cortex* 3(1967):163-78.

Kogan, N. "Educational Implications of Cognitive Styles." In *Psychology and Educational Practice,* edited by S. Lesser. Glenview, Ill.: Scott, Foresman, 1972.

Kogan, N., and Wallach, M.A. *Risk Taking: A Study in Cognition and Personality.* New York: Holt, Rinehart and Winston, 1964.

Languis, M.L. *Simultaneous and Successive Processing.* Unpublished concept paper prepared for NASSP Learning Styles Task Force, January 1983.

Lawrence, G. *People Types and Tiger Stripes.* Gainesville, Fla.: Center for Application of Psychological Type, 1979.

Leslie, H.P., et al. *Field Sensitive and Field Independent Teaching Strategies: New Approaches to Bilingual Bicultural Education, No. 5.* HEW-sponsored teaching manual from the Dissemination Center for Bilingual Bicultural Education, Austin, Texas, 1974.

Letteri, C.A. "Cognitive Profile: Basic Determinant of Academic Achievement." *Journal of Educational Research,* March/April 1980, pp. 195-99.

Levy, J. "Psychobiological Implications of Bilateral Asymmetry." In *Hemispheric Function in the Human Brain,* edited by S. Diamond and G. Beaumonts. New York: Halsted Press, 1974.

_____."Children Think with Whole Brains: Myth and Reality." In *Student Learning Styles and Brain Behavior — Programs, Instrumentation, Research.* Reston, Va.: NASSP, 1982.

_____. "Right Brain, Left Brain: Fact and Fiction." *Human Intelligence* 3(1985):1-3.

Levy, J., and Trevarthen, C. "Metacontrol of Hemispheric Function in Human Split Brain Patients." *Journal of Experimental Psychology: Human Perception and Performance.* 2(1976):299-312.

Lewin, K. *Field Theory in Social Science.* New York: Harper and Row, 1951.

Lindelow, J. *The Emerging Science of Individualized Instruction — A Survey of Findings on Learning Styles, Brain Research, and Learning Time with Implications for Administrative Action.* Eugene, Oreg.: ERIC Clearinghouse on Educational Management, 1983.

Lowery, R.E. *Letteri's Information Processing Model as Related to Cognitive Structure.* Paper presented at the WJHMSPA Network Learning Styles/Brain Research Conference, Tacoma, Wash., 1982.

Luria, A.R. *The Working Brain — An Introduction to Neuropsychology.* New York: Basic Books, 1973.

Maccoby, E.E., and Jacklin, C.N. "What We Know and Don't Know About Sex Differences." *Psychology Today,* December 1974, pp. 109-12.

Maccoby, M. "A Psychoanalytic View of Learning." *Change* 3(1972):32-

38.

Marcus, L. "A Comparison of Selected 9th Grade Male and Female Students' Learning Styles." *The Journal* (School Administrators Association of New York) 7(1977):27-28.

Martin, M.K. "Effects of the Interaction Between Students' Learning Styles and High School Instructional Environments." Doctoral dissertation, University of Oregon, 1977.

Maslow, A.H. *Toward a Psychology of Being,* 2nd ed. Princeton, N.J.: Van Nostrand, 1968.

McCarthy, B. *The 4MAT System.* Oak Brook, Ill.: EXCEL, 1980.

McClelland, D.C.; Atkinson, J.W.; Clark, R.A.; and Lowell, E.L. *The Achievement Motive.* New York: Appleton, 1955.

McGuinness, D. "How Schools Discriminate Against Boys." *Human Nature,* February 1979, 82-88.

McKenney, J.L., and Keen, P.G.W. "How Managers' Minds Work." *Harvard Business Review* 53(1974):79-90.

Messick, S., and Associates. *Individuality in Learning.* San Francisco: Jossey-Bass, 1976.

National Association of Secondary School Principals. *Student Learning Styles — Diagnosing and Prescribing Programs.* Reston, Va.: NASSP, 1979.

———. *Student Learning Styles and Brain Behavior — Programs, Instrumentation, Research.* Reston, Va.: NASSP, 1982.

Ornstein, R. *The Psychology of Consciousness.* New York: Viking Press, 1972.

Pettigrew, T.F. "The Measurement and Correlates of Category Width as a Cognitive Variable." *Journal of Personality* 26(1958):532-44.

Ramirez, M., III et al. *Introduction to Cognitive Styles: New Approaches to Bilingual Bicultural Education, No. 3.* HEW-sponsored teaching manual from the Dissemination Center for Bilingual Bicultural Education, Austin, Texas, 1974.

Reinert, H. "One Picture Is Worth a Thousand Words? Not Necessarily!" *Modern Language Journal,* April 1976, pp. 160-68.

Riessman, F. *The Culturally Deprived Child.* New York: Harper and Row, 1962.

Rotter, J.B. "Generalized Expectancies for Internal Versus External Control of Reinforcements." *Psychological Monographs* 80(1966):1-28.

———."External Control and Internal Control." *Psychology Today,* June 1971, pp. 37-42.

Scott, W.A. "Cognitive Complexity and Cognitive Flexibility." *Sociometry* 25(1962):405-14.

Sinatra, R., and Stahl-Gemake, J. *Using the Right Brain in the Language Arts.* Springfield, Ill.: Charles C. Thomas, 1983.

Skinner, B.F. *Science and Human Behavior.* New York: Macmillan, 1953.

Sperry, L. *Learning Performance and Individual Differences.* Glenview, Ill.: Scott, Foresman, 1972.

———."Counselors and Learning Styles." *Personnel and Guidance Journal*

51(1973):478-83.

Spielberger, C.D., ed. *Anxiety and Behavior.* New York: Academic Press, 1966.

Springer, S.P., and Deutsch, G. *Left Brain, Right Brain.* San Francisco: W. H. Freeman, 1981.

Thelen, H. *Dynamics of Groups at Work.* Chicago: University of Chicago Press, 1954.

Thornell, J.G. "Individual Differences in Cognitive Styles and the Guidance Variable in Instruction." *The Journal of Experimental Education* 42(1973):59-63.

Waterhouse, I.K., and Child, I. "Frustration and the Quality of Performance." *Journal of Personality* 21(1953):298-311.

Weil, M.L., and Murphy, J. "Instruction Processes." In *Encyclopedia of Educational Research,* 5th ed., edited by H.E. Mitzel. New York: The Free Press, 1982.

Witkin, H.A.; Lewis, H.G.; Hertzman, M.; Machover, K.; Meisener, P.B.; and Wapner, S. *Personality Through Perception.* New York: Harper, 1954.

Witkin, H.A.; Oltman, P.K.; Raskin, E.; and Karp, S.S. *A Manual for the Embedded Figures Test.* Palo Alto, Calif.: Consulting Psychologists Press, 1971.

Wittig, M.A., and Peterson, A.C., eds. *Sex-Related Differences in Cognitive Functioning — Developmental Issues.* New York: Academic Press, 1979.

Wittrock, M.C., ed. *The Brain and Psychology.* New York: Academic Press, 1980.

Witty, P. "A Study of Children's Interests: Grades 9, 10, 11, 12." *Education* 82(1961):39-45, 100-10, 169-74.

Yando, R.M., and Kagan, J. "The Effect of Teacher Tempo on the Child." *Child Development* 39(1968):27-34.